IONA

A Celebration

For centuries Iona has exerted a fascination out of all proportion to its diminutive size and annually attracts thousands who make the pilgrimage to Columba's Isle. Lying off the west coast of Scotland it has been a cradle for northern Christianity for over fifteen centuries and is also the legendary burial-place of Scottish, Irish and Norwegian kings.

Like countless others, John L. Paterson was captivated by the spirit of Iona. He decided to celebrate the unique qualities of the island not only in words but in photographs which have proved to be superbly evocative. Together, the text and the black-and-white images offer a companionable guide to the visitor exploring Iona for the first time and a splendid souvenir, guaranteed to revive vivid recollections of a walk round the island. In addition, this book will whet the appetite of all who have yet to set foot on this, the most historic of all Scotland's Western Isles.

JOHN L. PATERSON is Principal of Edinburgh College of Art. He is also an architect and exhibition designer whose work includes the Landmark Visitor Centre at Carrbridge and the Grange Arts Centre at Oldham. He is consultant architect/designer to the PSA for the new Theatre Museum at Covent Garden, London.

IONA

*A Celebration
by John L Paterson*

John Murray

To my aunt, Dora Paterson,
with whom I first visited Iona many years ago

Illustrations 1–8 and 10 in the text are in the possession of the Iona Community and are reproduced by kind permission of the Iona Cathedral Trust. Illustrations 9 and 11 in the text, and included on the front cover, are reproduced by kind permission of the Board of Trinity College, Dublin. Map of Iona is by Denys Baker.

TECHNICAL NOTE: The two cameras used were a Rolleiflex 3003 35 mm and a Hasselblad SWC/M; film used: Ilford FP4–120, XP1–120 and Kodak Panatomic X–35 mm.

© John L. Paterson 1987

First published 1987
by John Murray (Publishers) Ltd
50 Albemarle Street, London W1X 4BD

Typeset, printed and bound in Great Britain
by Butler & Tanner Ltd, Frome and London

British Library Cataloguing in Publication Data
Paterson, John L.
  Iona: a celebration.
  1. Iona (Scotland)——Description and
  travel——Views
  I. Title
  941.4′23   DA880.I7
  ISBN 0-7195-4306-1

Preface

Among the many visitors to Iona there have been writers, painters and photographers who have provided us with a record of their impressions but none, as far as I know, who has placed an equal emphasis upon words and images to convey a response to the island. This I have attempted to do, since words alone cannot communicate the extraordinary quality of light which, in certain conditions and times of the day, has a luminosity that appears to suspend the island in another dimension of space. But then neither can images detail adequately the inspired history of Iona as a spiritual centre of religious belief for nearly two millenniums. However, even with a combination of text and photographs I doubt if I have been able to encompass the unique qualities that the island possesses and which can be properly appreciated only by visiting the island and discovering it for yourself, as I have done.

This book is not only a celebration of those qualities, it is also a personal interpretation of the island and I am grateful for the opportunity given to me to study its history and record its landscape, so gaining an insight into the nature of religious belief as revealed within the microcosm of the natural world that is Iona.

I would like to record my debt to a number of friends and colleagues without whose generous support very little would ever have materialised: to Cathy Aitken, who inspired the enterprise and who also confirmed or corrected my speculations; to Fiona Gardner, who conjured legibility from an indecipherable manuscript; to George Hutchison, who magically drew light and shadows from my recalcitrant images; to Jenny Law, who successfully directed me towards a sympathetic publisher; and, finally, to Ian Bowles and Robin Drummond-Hay, who provided a gastronomic haven at Ardfenaig from which I could foray among the elements. To each and all, including the people of Iona, I offer my gratitude, with the hope that my debt to them may be partially repaid in what has been published.

John L. Paterson
Edinburgh
June 1986

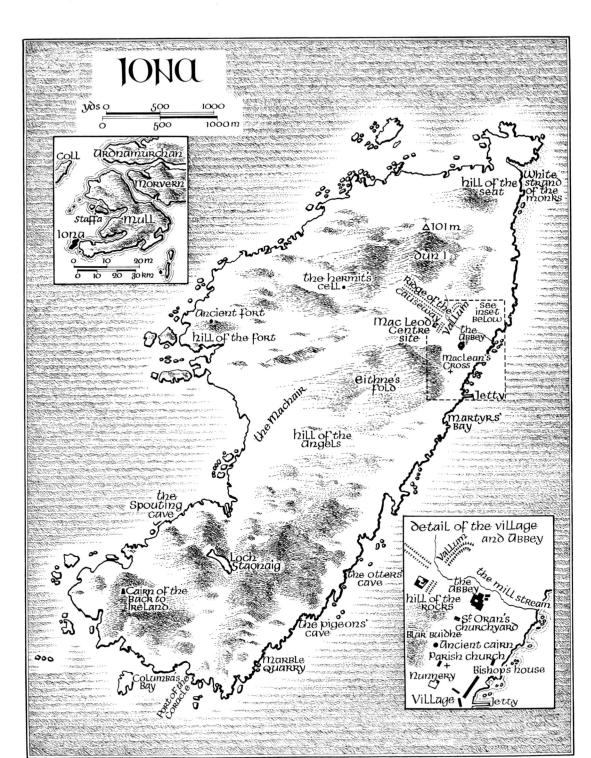

IONA

yds 0 — 500 — 1000
0 — 500 — 1000 m

COLL
ARONAMURCHAN
MORVERN
STAFFA — MULL
IONA
0 — 10 — 20 m
0 — 10 — 20 — 30 km

hill of the seat
White strand of the monks
△101 m
dun I
the hermits cell
Ridge of the causeway
vallum
see inset below
MacLeod Centre site
the Abbey
Maclean's Cross
Ancient fort
hill of the fort
Eithne's fold
jetty
the Machair
Martyrs' Bay
hill of the angels
the Spouting cave
detail of the village and Abbey
vallum
the mill stream
the Abbey
hill of the rocks
St Oran's churchyard
Blar Buidhe
Ancient cairn
Parish church
Nunnery
Bishops house
village
jetty
Loch Staonaig
the otters cave
Cairn of the Back to Ireland
the pigeons' cave
MARBLE QUARRY
Columba's Bay
Port of the Coracle

You first glimpse the island of Iona as you drive over the hill and down to the ferry terminal at Fionnphort on Mull. Across the Sound, less than a mile from you, lies the island. Three miles in length, north to south and half that at its widest, its highest point is the summit of Dun I some 330 ft above sea-level; nevertheless, Iona does not possess any particular physical character that would distinguish it from a hundred other such islands. Then your eye catches sight of a large building that lies near the foot of Dun I. It is the Abbey, and the reason – in all probability – for your travelling for three hours from Oban to visit this place. That an obscure little island off the west coast of Scotland should have become known throughout Christendom during the early middle ages is attributable to one man, St Columba, but it is a cause for wonder that it has remained so for well over fifteen centuries. It may come as something of a surprise to many visitors that Columba's mission in *c*. 563 predated Augustine's arrival at Canterbury by some thirty years.

The ferry takes only a few minutes to cross the Sound of Iona and most visitors immediately set off to walk up the hill past the village towards the Abbey – no longer a ruin, but completely restored by the Iona Community. You can spend the whole of your short visit at the Abbey and its ancillary buildings, but this would be a pity because there is so much else to see on the island.

I would suggest, if you have the time and you wish to experience for yourself something of the unusual atmosphere that the island is said to possess, that when you step onto the shore from the ferry you do not follow the other visitors, but set off instead towards the southern end of the island. Taking the south road you will first pass Martyrs' Bay, a small beach-fringed cove, where, in 806, Vikings on one of their periodic raids on the island butchered sixty-eight monks. It was this attack on the monastery that forced the monks to abandon the island and to settle permanently at Kells in County Meath, Ireland. It is appropriate, therefore, that at this bay the Street of the Dead began, the route for many early Scottish noblemen who were to be buried in state within the grounds of Iona Abbey. There is also at Martyrs' Bay a memorial to two world wars where the names of twenty-seven islanders are commemorated. And if you look up from the memorial you will often see on a clear day the exhaust trails from aircraft at cirrus altitudes, contrails like pennants flowing from the Horsemen of the Apocalypse, for these are frequently Soviet Bear or American F-111 bombers maintaining a precarious peace which has lasted, so far, for four decades.

Hill of the Angels and the Machair

The road from the bay follows the sea for a short distance and then turns abruptly west climbing over the ridge that runs along the central part of the island. On the far side lies the Machair, an area of comparatively flat land, now a small golf-course, but which was once cultivated by the monks as the ground was sufficiently fertile to raise crops. However, before you reach it you pass on your left a large mound known as *Cnoc nan Aingeal*, Hill of the Angels. Here, legend has it, Columba was once surrounded by Angels descended from Heaven. The Hill of the Angels is also the fairy hill where pagan custom received Christian consent. Here, late in September, on the eve of St Michael's Day, the islanders brought their horses to circle the hill. As the zoologist and traveller Thomas Pennant described it during a visit to the island in the late eighteenth century: 'Round this hill they all made the turn sunwise, thus unwittingly dedicating their horses to the sun.'

1 Horses swimming to Mull, c.1890

Light and shadow, Christian belief and pagan ritual, two apparently conflicting forces that appear very often to be interchangeable in the history of the island, even to the present century. One night in the early years of this century, a woman, a visitor to the island, living near the fairy hill, slipped naked out of the cottage in which she was staying with a knife in her hand to cut open the hill presumably to free its inhabitants. She was found dead the next morning and is buried in *Reilig Orain*, St Oran's Churchyard.

The road ends at the Machair but there is a track that leads to the edge of the Atlantic where the horizon is broken only by a series of small islands almost all of which are identical in shape – steep-sided, but flat in outline except for one, Dutchman's Cap, from which rises a conical hill that gives the island its unique profile. The others have more romantic names – Fladda, Gometra, Lunga, Staffa, Ulva – but this island, with its unusual geological formation, must have been a more useful landmark than the others for ships sailing from the west through the archipelago to Iona.

It was along the seashore of the Machair at midnight before Maundy Thursday (the Thursday before Easter) of each year that the population of Iona, like other Western Islanders, would make an offering to the sea-god Shony. The ancient custom of *Diardaoin a Brochain Mhoir*, Great Gruel Thursday, was enacted on Iona until the end of the eighteenth century. A man would wade into the ocean pouring from a container either mead, gruel or ale as an offering to the sea believing, in return, that it would provide a plentiful supply of seaweed to fertilise the second ploughing of spring.

To the south-west of the Machair, beyond a small beach, the ground rises rapidly, forming a cliff-face to the Atlantic. There are a number of small caves, the most prominent of which is *Uamh an t-Seididh*, Spouting Cave, where, if a heavy sea is running, a fountain of water bursts above the ground in a spectacular display of aquatic pyrotechnics.

The Port of the Coracle

There are no footpaths in this rock-strewn landscape, but further inland there is a well-trodden path which forms a natural route to the high ground where Loch Staonaig is situated. This is now a reservoir and provides a water supply for the islanders. On the far side of the loch the ground falls gently down to the southern edge of the island. It is here, so it is said, that Columba first stepped ashore with twelve followers on 12 May 563, having sailed 100 miles to the east of Ireland in order to 'seek the place of one's resurrection' rather than to proselytise the faith in Alba among the Picts and Scots of Dalriada. Tradition plays a powerful part in the story of Iona and beliefs, handed down by word of mouth from one generation to another, are an essential feature of the continuing life of this remote community. It is tradition of this kind that is the strongest evidence for Columba's residence on the island. In addition to the tradition there is the significance of the names of many places, which may or may not locate accurately the known historical facts of the missionary's life on Iona. But one strange feature which has to do with the consequence of words, and which is an unusual coincidence, is that *columba* is the Latin for dove, which is *Iona* in Hebrew, and legend has it that Columba arrived on the eve of Pentecost, and the symbol of Pentecost is a dove. The doves that circle the Abbey are a rare – if not unique – breed, descendants of the wild rock pigeon.

Columba, the tradition has it, landed on a pebbled beach known to this day as the Port of the Coracle, strewn like a ransacked jewel-casket with stones of quartz, marble, feldspar, hornblende, epidote and slate.

Why did Columba come to Iona, and did he land on the island merely by chance? Although very little is known of Columba's early career in Ireland, it is thought that he was involved in 561 in the Battle of Cùl Dreimne, fought between factions within the royal house of Uí Neill of which Columba's own clan, Conaill, was a part – and that he was held responsible for instigating the conflict. Whatever the truth of this accusation, Columba was excommunicated the following year by a Synod of Irish Clergy, which, although temporary, may have been the cause of his self-imposed exile in 563.

There was also the tradition of the Irish Celtic Church in the fifth and sixth centuries for 'peregrinatio', or wandering, that had its antecedents in the second and third centuries when thousands of early Christians, persecuted by the Romans, sought refuge in the Egyptian desert. An ideal grew from these 'desert fathers', that of seeking a simpler life of contemplation, and in so doing rejected the temptations of the world by fasting and self-mortification. This asceticism developed uniquely in the Irish Church to be realised in the Anchorite movement that emerged in the first half of the eighth century, and Columba was certainly an early follower of that movement. Adomnan, in his Life of the Saint, wrote that Columba left Ireland for Scotland 'pro christo peregrinari volens enavigerit' and that he was, like many other religious leaders, 'seeking the place of one's resurrection'.

To the west of the Port of the Coracle is a hill named *Carn Cul ri Eirinn*, literally Cairn of the Back to Ireland, and is the hill, it is claimed, that Columba climbed to reassure himself that he could no longer see Ireland after landing on Iona. Whatever the reason or reasons that led Columba to settle on Iona must, in the end, remain a matter for speculation. There is insufficient evidence to reach a definite conclusion, particularly where fact too readily shades into legend. What may be surmised, however, is that Columba was probably aware of the existence of the island as part of the Dalriada kingdom and, possibly, had obtained a description of its potential as a sanctuary for himself and his companions. The ground was sufficiently fertile to raise crops; the eastern shore was protected from Atlantic storms by a ridge of hills which provided spring water and there was an adequate area of even ground on which to build adjacent to a point where a ferry crossing could be made across the Sound to Mull.

Retracing one's steps along the route to the coracle, it is worth reflecting that in all probability Columba would have followed the same path towards the hinterland of the island.

For the adventurous it is possible to strike eastwards across the moorland to explore along the coastline and discover the marble quarry, abandoned in 1914, or the pigeon or otter caves. But for me the pleasure is to walk over the plain towards the north, losing all sight of human occupation and to be aware of the three elements – earth, sky and sea – which not only provide a constant reflection on the temporal nature of man, but also an awareness of infinity. There are other parts of the island which are possibly more beautiful but none that suggests with such directness the inconsequence of time as a measure of existence.

Eithne's Fold and the Nunnery

And then, without warning, after climbing over a final ridge the whole of the north of the island is before you. To the west is the Machair; to the east the village with the clear outline of the Abbey in the far distance; and on the horizon the red Caledonian Granite coastline of the Ross of Mull. Ahead of you, a mile and a half away, is Dun I. Below you is a farm with a path that becomes a track leading to Dun I. The track joins the road which connects the Machair to the village, but instead of joining it cross over and follow the continuous track towards a second farm at the brow of a hill. Adjacent to it there is some grazing pasture called *Bol Leithne* or Eithne's Fold. This was the point midway between the Abbey and the Machair which the monks used to pass each day on their way to and from their work in the fields.

Adomnan recalls in his biography of Columba, written nearly a century after the Saint's death, that the monks became aware one evening after harvesting the crops of a strange and unusual presence in Eithne's Fold, and this experience occurred again on subsequent days at the same hour each evening. One elder brother, describing the incident, said that he could 'perceive the fragrance of such a wonderful odour, just as if all the flowers on earth were gathered together in one place; I feel also a glow of heat within me – not at all painful – but most pleasing – and a certain unusual and unexplainable joy poured into my heart, which all of a sudden so refreshes and gladdens me I forget grief and weariness of every kind. Even the load, however heavy, which I carry on my back is in some mysterious way so much lightened, from this place all the way to the monastery, that I do not seem to have any weight to bear.'

'All the other reapers in turn', records Adomnan, 'declared that they had exactly the same feeling.' When they asked a fellow monk, Baithen, what it all meant he declared that it was the spirit of Columba that had returned to comfort them since in life he had always grieved when they returned later than usual to the monastery.

This story is typical of many such legends. Virtually every part of Iona has a history attached to it that may be recounted to the visitor. This is not surprising for the island is small, the paths well trodden, and in the numerous and descriptive names of the inlets and hills – names which remain to this day – there is that Celtic delight in immortalising the small events of history which led to designating those places on the island where events occurred, which might otherwise have remained unrecognised and forgotten.

Continuing your journey along the track you will pass the ruins of a nunnery originally founded within the first decade of the thirteenth century by Reginald, son of Somerled, ruler of the isles. Built as a house for Augustinian nuns, or canonesses, it may possibly owe its existence to Reginald's sister, Beatrice, who was the first prioress of the nunnery. Although it is in a ruinous condition and has been only partially restored, nevertheless it is one of the finest examples in the United Kingdom of this type of building.

The Old Village and Distinguished Visitors

Adjacent to the site of the nunnery is the village. The buildings are of fairly recent origin and quite different in appearance from those photographed by the Edinburgh surgeon and amateur photographer Dr Thomas Keith in September 1856. Nevertheless, this part of Iona has for centuries provided the main settlement for the island's community, although unfortunately such evidence as exists on the history of Iona refers almost exclusively to the history of the Christian Church on the island, so that very little is known of the early secular population.

There is archaeological evidence of pre-Columban occupation, but no verification of the existence of an island community, apart from the monastery, until the sixteenth century. However, in the precincts of the nunnery there is a medieval parish church, St Ronan's, which was abandoned with the restoration of the Abbey by Charles I in the 1630s; this suggests that there was a sufficiently large lay settlement to justify a parsonage, first referred to in 1372.

In 1561 it was recorded that dues were paid by tenants for rental of land, and in *Highland*

2 Iona from the beach, photographed by Dr Thomas Keith, September 1856

Papers of Donald Gregory (1674) there is a reference to Iona as being 'possest be tenants, and pays only this yeir of money £160, of bear [barley] 30 bolls'. This amount has been estimated as having been produced by a population of several hundred.

In the seventeenth century the Synod of Argyll met on two occasions on Iona, in 1642 and 1656, and on the second occasion it was proposed to repair the fabric of the Abbey and establish a school on Iona to educate the sons of the noblemen of Mull, Morven, Coll and Tiree; but in the end nothing came of the proposals and the Abbey became gradually more ruinous as a result. In 1685 a visitor could comment that 'The altar is large, and of as fine marble as ever I saw,' but by 1760 it was in fragments because 'the common people break pieces of it' using them as 'cures' for human and animal diseases.

Thomas Pennant, visiting the island in 1772, noted in his *Voyage to the Hebrides* that of the altar 'only a very small portion is now left, and even that we continued to diminish'. He also mentioned that 'the number of inhabitants is about a hundred and fifty; the most stupid and the most lazy of all the islanders'. At the time of Pennant's visit the majority of the islanders were living in the village which he described as 'consisting at present of about fifty houses, mostly very mean, thatched with straw of bear pulled up at the roots, and bound tight on the roof with ropes made of heath. Some of the houses that lie a little beyond the rest seemed to have been better constructed than the others, and to have been the mansions of the inhabitants when the place was in a flourishing state, but at present are in a very ruinous condition.'

A year later, in October 1773, Dr Johnson and James Boswell visited the island and Johnson noted: 'The village near the churches is said to contain seventy families, which, at five in a family, is more than a hundred inhabitants to a mile. There are perhaps other villages; yet

12

*3 Thatching a croft on Iona,
c. 1914*

both corn and cattle are annually exported. But the fruitfulness of Iona is now its whole prosperity. The inhabitants are remarkably gross, and remarkably neglected: I know not if they are visited by any minister. The island, which was once the metropolis of learning and piety, has now no school for education, nor temple for worship; only two inhabitants can speak English, and not one that can write or read.' After describing the dilapidated state of the Bishop's house, Johnson continues: 'There is in the island one house more, and only one, that has a chimney; we entered it, and found it neither wanting repair, nor inhabitants; but to the farmers, who now possess it, the chimney is of no great value, for their fire was made on the floor in the middle of the room and, notwithstanding the dignity of their mansion, they rejoiced, like their neighbours, in the comforts of smoke.'

It should be pointed out that at that time Iona was, in fact, visited every six weeks by a minister from the Ross of Mull, who conducted his services in a private house.

Johnson and Boswell were followed to Iona twenty-three years later, in 1786, by the redoubtable Sarah Murray, a widow, who, at the age of fifty-two, set out on a tour of some 2000 miles around Scotland: 'Cattle are fed on I-Columbkill, but sheep are forbidden by the proprietor on account of the smallness of the island. A very few sheep are, however, reared on I-Ona; but it is in secret. There are no trees on the island, nor fuel of any sort. At the proper season the inhabitants cross over to Ross, where they find plenty of peat mosses. From these mosses, or black bogs, they cut, dry and pile vast quantities of peat, and let them remain in stacks upon the mosses until completely fit for use; they then set all their boats and hands to work to convey their yearly store of fuel across the Sound to their houses.... The good woman

13

at the inn at I-Ona, when we returned from our long and fatiguing peregrination, furnished us with a meal of fine fish and excellent potatoes; hunger added the best of sauce. When our dinner was concluded, the young ladies of our party and I went down to the bay; while we were seated on the rocks impending over the bay, numbers of women and children came after us, and by degrees some of the old ones crept from one piece of rock to another, until they were close to us. The men and boys kept a respectful distance, not that they had less curiosity, but were more bashful than the women. The manners of the females appeared to me to be innocent, simple, and crouching like spaniel dogs approaching their masters. If fear had not deterred them, I verily believe the poor things would have gladly fondled us. Very seldom indeed are their eyes accustomed to look upon strangers of either sex, and a few shillings distributed amongst them afforded a transient joy not easily described.'

The Duke of Argyll's factor in 1789 reported that 'strangers are much hurt at seeing so much neglected'. The Duke ordered the ruins to be enclosed behind a stone wall with a locked gate under the supervision of the schoolmaster, the position having been established in 1775. The need to protect the Abbey was the result of the tenants removing stones from the building for the construction of their own houses, while continuing to use the ruins as a byre. The nunnery was equally neglected, since it served as a cowshed.

It appears that by 1819 there was a minister in residence on Iona, although the island was still without a parish church. A letter from the Reverend Leigh Richmond to his wife in that year reveals: 'Iona is delightful! You can form no idea of the characteristics of everything and everybody around me. The novelty, simplicity, and singularity – the tout ensemble – is indescribable. Here, amid the ruins of ancient grandeur, piety and literature, surrounded by the graves and mouldering grave-stones of kings, chieftains, lords of the isles, bishops, priests, abbesses, nuns, and friars – the sense decorated with the fine and romantic remains of cathedral, colleges, nunnery, chapels, and oratories; with views of islands, seas, rocks, mountains, interspersed with the humble huts of these poor islanders! I am just preparing to preach to as many of them as can understand English, in the open air; a rock my pulpit, and Heaven my sounding-board; may the echo resound to their hearts.'

Reference has already been made to the appointment of a schoolmaster in 1775 and there is an interesting comment made by Lachlan Maclean that 'The fair sex – last at the cross, and first at the grave – have not been unmindful of the needs of Iona. In the summer of 1832, the sum of £25 was collected by an English lady, and placed in the hands of the minister, Mr Campbell, for the establishment of an infant school. It is now begun with every prospect of success. I am also informed that an Edinburgh lady has this summer collected £27 for the same object. But their school-book, which must be in Gaelic, poor urchins, is only in manuscript still! Not because we have no printers in Scotland. I may not omit to mention, also, that some of the first Ladies in the Highlands are coadjutors in this work: but I have no authority to give names; pleased with their fame in Heaven, they care not for my praise.'

Because of the relatively poor economy of Iona, attempts were made by the Argyll estates to encourage new industries to the island such as fisheries, flax spinning and marble quarrying, but these did not prove to be very successful.

However, the fame of Iona began to spread among a newly interested public in the late eighteenth century and by the middle of the nineteenth there were regular sailings from Oban, giving rise to an important element of the island's economy: tourism. As a result many distinguished visitors have recorded their impressions over the years providing cameos of the island, revealing momentarily the life of the community. I have already quoted Dr Johnson, Thomas Pennant and Sarah Murray all writing in the late eighteenth century. Then in 1810 Sir Walter Scott visited Iona and wrote to George Ellis: 'The inhabitants are in the last state of poverty and wretchedness. Fisheries might relieve them, but I see no other resource, for the island, though fertile, considering all things, does not produce food for the inhabitants, and they have neither money nor commodities to induce importation of provisions.'

In 1818 Keats noted on his visit that 'The old schoolmaster, who is an ignorant little man but reckoned very clever, showed us these things – he is a Macklean and as much above 4 foot as he is under 4 foot 3 inches – he stops at one glass of whisky unless you press another and at the second unless you press a third.'

Mendelssohn on his tour of the islands in 1829 revealed a sympathy, unusual at that time, for a community faced with the onslaught of tourism: 'If I had my home on Iona, and lived there upon melancholy as other people do upon their rents, my darkest moment would be when in that wide space, that deals in nothing but cliffs and sea-gulls, suddenly a curl of steam should appear, followed by a ship and finally by a gay party in veils and frock-coats, which would look for an hour at the ruins and graves and the three little huts for the living, and then move off again. This highly unjustifiable joke, occurring twice a week, and being almost the only thing to make one aware that there are such things as time and clocks in the world, would be as if the inhabitants of these old graves haunted the place in a ludicrous disguise. Opposite Iona stands a rocky island which, to complete the effect, looks like a ruined city.'

Ruin was indeed to follow. Iona, like other parts of the Western Isles, had come to depend almost entirely for its subsistence on the potato crop. This failed in 1846 and for some years following. In 1847 the Destitution Committee of the Free Churches reported: 'In Iona and the Ross of Mull, they found more sickness prevailing than elsewhere – fever, dysentery and a particular type of typhus fever.'

A Mr Donald Maclean, a merchant of Bunessan, wrote to the committee on 13 January 1847: 'There are several families in this district actually in a dying state from starvation and sickness. Families consisting of from six to nine children, besides parents, and days without anything to eat except shell-fish and sea-ware, except when relieved by a handful of meal from those who have some; and what I have stated is little of what I have witnessed in visiting some of the families. I sincerely trust, whatever supplies the committee may send to this place may be sent as speedily as can be by any means. The sickness is so great, with other calamities, that the number of deaths some days are between Ross and Iona from two to five. I am sorry to add, that sickness is still on the increase, particularly British cholera and dysentery.'

With an unerring sense of royal timing, Queen Victoria anchored off-shore from Iona in August of the same year, as reported in the *Imperial Gazetteer*: 'Prince Albert, the Prince of Leinengen, the Duke of Norfolk, Earl Grey and Sir James Clark landed on the island, while the

4 *Iona Abbey, photographed at some time between 1860 and 1900*

5 *Iona village, c. 1890*

16

Queen herself was contiguous on the royal yacht, at the time of the progress northward to Ardverike; and they had a reception from the people as primitive and decorous as was probably given anywhere to any ancient Lord of the Isles. A few plainly dressed islanders stood on the shore, carrying tufted willow-wands, and prepared to act as an escort; the body of the people, for the most part decently dressed, stood behind, looking eagerly on as spectators, yet all maintaining a respectful distance; only a few children, in the usual fashion of the island, offered pebbles and shells for sale; and when the august visitors, after quietly surveying the curiosities of the place, returned to the barge, all the population gave loud voice in a hearty farewell cheer.'

Two worlds met for a moment, uncomprehending, and passed their separate ways.

In 1779 the population was 249 of whom sixty-one were male; by 1842 it had increased to about 500; but by 1861 had dropped to 264, as a result of malnutrition, disease and emigration – by those healthy enough to leave what was later to be called 'a deserted necropolis'. The population continued to decline and at the third Statistical Account of 1951 it was estimated at a little over 100 people, at which figure it has remained to the present day.

Credit should be given to the eighth Duke of Argyll, who, during the course of his lifetime, laid the foundations for the restoration of the Abbey buildings and the improvement of the living standards of the island community. One of his last public acts was to make in 1899 a deed of gift which secured for the Church of Scotland the possession of the Abbey and nunnery ruins. He died the following year.

The Village Today

A link with the past which provides a fitting testimonial to the resilience of the people of Iona over a period of at least eight centuries is in the person of Miss Mary Maclean. I was privileged to take her photograph three days before her hundredth birthday in 1984. I was also able to photograph other members of the island community: the Abbey groundsmen, the postmistress, an island boatman, a villager, a beekeeper, the parish minister, now sadly retired, leaving the island without a resident preacher, and finally the children at the school which gave me the greatest pleasure since they confirm, as a future generation, the continuing vitality of the people of Iona. All those whom I photographed displayed the natural courtesy which is characteristic of the Western Islander. The casual visitor, in his fashionable haste, hardly notices them for the islanders do not obtrude in their daily lives on the passing traveller.

If you walk down the village street you will soon realise that the community can now maintain itself to a standard and quality of life that was impossible to imagine only three generations ago. The well-maintained houses with their neatly trimmed gardens on the opposite side of the road reflect the changes that have taken place on the island. Tourism has obviously played a part in all this but the major improvements on Iona have been achieved as a result of the efforts of the islanders with some support from the state which has at long last taken a greater interest in the well-being of the Western Isles, providing some small compensation for the disgraceful neglect of the islands by successive governments in the past.

Iona Post Office, c. 1890–5,
sited differently from present day

You can continue your journey towards the Abbey along a path at the end of the village street which will take you past the Bishop's house. This was built by Bishop Neil Campbell in the 1630s when an unsuccessful attempt was made to restore the Abbey as the Cathedral of the Isles. A comment by Dr Johnson, referred to earlier, indicated the state of disrepair which it had reached by 1773. There is also a path half-way along the street adjacent to the Argyll Hotel which brings you onto the road to the Abbey, and not far from here you will see the thin, weather-beaten stone of MacLean's Cross, erected by a member of that clan in the latter part of the fifteenth century. The cross marks the junction of the three medieval streets which linked the two former landing stages of the island with the Abbey and nunnery. Behind the cross is the Parish Church and Manse, built in 1828 to a standard design of Thomas Telford.

Further up the road you will pass St Columba's Hotel and 200 yds to the west of the hotel buildings, although not marked by any path to its location, is a small, grass-covered mound known as *Blar Buihde*; this is thought to be a burial cairn of about 2000 BC and is one of the few prehistoric sites that have been discovered on the island. Another is on *Dun Bhuirg* at the north end of the Machair where there are the remains of an Iron Age dun or hill-fort, one of many around the Western Isles, which dates from between the first century BC and third century AD, built presumably for protection against the warring tribes of the area.

Whoever lived on the island is not certain, but it is likely that they were hunters, fishermen and food-gatherers. Nor is anyone certain whether the island was ever used for druidic worship. The old druidic Stone of Destiny, forcibly removed by Edward I in 1296 to Westminster Abbey as part of the Coronation Throne, is said to be one of the Black Stones of Iona, so called not

7 *MacLean's Cross, c. 1900*

because of their colour but because of the fate that befell anyone who violated an oath sworn upon them. The stones were described by Martin Martin in the seventeenth century as being sited to the west of *Dun nai Monach*. Unfortunately, however, the last of these stones disappeared in the nineteenth century and no trace now remains of them. Neil M. Gunn, in his book *Off in a Boat* (1938), does mention that until recently Highlanders still referred to Iona as the 'Druids' Isle' and that at one time there were a number of standing stones together with a druidic temple of twelve stones, but there is no evidence to support his claim.

Reilig Orain and the Monastery

Twenty-five yards from the hotel along the road to the Abbey stands a sycamore, one of the few trees on the island, with its branches spreading over a corner of the island's burial-ground, *Reilig Orain*, St Oran's Churchyard. This dates from the early Christian period although it is uncertain whether *Reilig Orain* formed part of the Columban monastery. It is also known as the burial-place of kings, and one of the kings of Dalriada, Fergus, is said to have been buried there, a generation before the arrival of Columba. It is also reputed to be the burial-place of forty-eight kings of Scotland, four Irish kings and eight Norwegian kings but as there is no evidence of their tombs to be found this may be another legend of the island, created possibly to give importance to long-forgotten chiefs of west Highland clans who are buried there.

Across the north wall of *Reilig Orain* can be seen a recently excavated section of the Street of the Dead. As was mentioned earlier this started at Martyrs' Bay ending at the door of the Abbey. Walking over the rough stones of the small section of excavated roadway within the precinct of the Abbey provides a possible insight into the symbolic intentions of the creators of the Street of the Dead, the painful journey through life towards redemption in death. The road passes close to the original location of the first monastic buildings which have been identified by Professor Charles Thomas, based on excavations just south of the Abbey where he discovered the foundations of some of the buildings. The only remains of the original

19

8 *Unknown artist's impression of St Columba's Monastery, sixth century*

monastery still existing above ground consist of a *vallum* or rampart, typical of the period, which formed its symbolic and legal boundary. The ruins of this *vallum*, which was constructed as an earthwork surrounding an area of approximately 20 acres, can still be seen to the north and west of the present Abbey, and the remainder has been traced as having originally formed a rectangle centred on *Torr Abb*, Abbot's Tor, immediately to the west of the Abbey.

In *Celtic Scotland* (1886) Professor W. F. Skene made some interesting deductions from a close textual study of Adomnan's Life of the Saint, although, unfortunately, he sites the original monastery too far north of the present Abbey as the result of a misinterpretation of the extent of the *vallum*. From references drawn from Adomnan, Skene suggested that the monastery contained: 'A refectory of considerable size in which was a fireplace and a vessel of water ... a *hospitium* or guest-chamber, which was wattled, and the houses, or cells of the monks, with the *plateola*, or little court, which they surrounded ... constructed of wood ... the church with its *exedra*, or side chamber ... an *oratorium*, which shows that it was *Duirthech* or an oak building. He [Adomnan] frequently alludes to the house, or cell, occupied by Columba himself, which he says was built of planks and placed on the highest part of the ground. This places Columba's cell on *Torr Abb* and certainly there are stone remains there, and it is the highest point within the *vallum*. Adomnan describes it as being near a small hillock, overlooking the monastery and this suggests *Cnoc nan Carnan*, Hill of the Rocks.

Skene also identifies the landing-place for the ferry crossing from Mull as *Port na Muinntir*, Port of the Community, and as a result of this he is able to locate the kiln for the Abbey, again from references in Adomnan, as being situated between Columba's cell on *Torr Abb* and the

20

harbour, and as it would have been used for baking bread and other food it would have been close to the refectory, although possibly outside the *vallum*. Further textual analysis by Skene reveals that the refectory contained a stone table where the *eulogia*, or blessed bread, was broken; that the stone was called either *Moelblatha* or *Blathnat*; and that there was 'prosperity on all food which should be placed upon it'. Skene goes on to describe the land beyond the precincts of the monastery: 'Outside of the *vallum*, or rampart, was the *bocetum*, or cow-house, mentioned by Adomnan; and the land on the east side of the island, south of the mill-stream, appears to have been used for pasture, while the fertile land forming the western part of the central plain, as well probably as the level land at the north end of the island, was used for tillage; and there appear to have been two granaries for storing the grain – one near the monastery, and the other close to the fields under tillage.'

The general assumption is that the settlement at Iona was built exclusively of timber, since there are no extant remains, which suggests that stone was not used in the construction of the buildings. As Iona consists mainly of rocks, with very few trees, this might appear to be a perverse conclusion, although it is true that stone churches were not typical of the period.

However, it has been suggested that the original name of Iona was the Island of Yews and if this was based on fact then timber would be an obvious choice as a building material for Columba and his companions to adopt. Moreover, in his biography of Columba Adomnan refers to an occasion when 'the holy man, living at the time in Iona, sought among the woodland a place far remote from men and fitting for prayer'. This does suggest that the island was well provided with trees in the sixth century, confirming that the early monastic buildings – like their counterparts in Ireland – would have been constructed of wood. This tradition continued until the eighth century when Celtic churches began to be constructed of stone.

Iona: A Centre of Christianity

That Iona, during the lifetime of Columba, became one of the great centres of northern Christianity on the site of such uncontrived primitive buildings, gives cause for reflection. The subsequent history of the Christian Church has depended more on hewn and modelled stone for the reputation of its beliefs, than did those early missionary settlers, who had only their simple piety and faith to sustain their religion, but this was of such an intensity that to this day it remains the apotheosis of Christian devotion to which so many have continued to aspire.

The monastic order of Columba's Church was divided into three classes: the Seniors, the older men who carried out the religious services of the church as well as reading and transcribing the Bible; the Working Brothers, younger men, who farmed, prepared the food for the others and also served in the workshops, and amongst whom Adomnan refers, in particular, to the *pincerna*, or butler, who was in charge of the refectory, and the *pistor*, or baker, who was a Saxon; the third class consisted of the *alumini*, or pupils. From various sources, including stone carvings and illuminated manuscripts, some impression can be gained of their appearance. They were tonsured from ear to ear so that their hair was allowed to grow only on the back of their heads. They wore a white *tunica*, or undergarment, over which was worn a *camilla* with a hood made of undyed wool. When working or travelling they wore sandals which they removed when meat was served, usually at the principal meal of the day, otherwise their diet consisted of bread, milk, fish, eggs and seal meat.

Divine worship, as practised on Iona and described by Adomnan, centred on the celebration of the Eucharist, which took place on Sundays, on the religious festivals of the Church and on particular days that the Abbot would determine. Adomnan referred to these services as 'the Sacred Mysteries of the Eucharist' or 'the Mysteries of the sacred oblation'. The main Christian festival of the year was Easter, the date of which remained a contentious issue between the Iona Church and the Catholic hierarchy until it was resolved in 716.

Monastic discipline was one of the most important features of daily life in Columba's time. Ordinary discipline consisted of fasting on Wednesdays, Fridays and during Lent, to which was added, for the more devout monks, total immersion of their bodies in water while they recited a part or the whole of the Psalter. If any offence was committed, the penitent had to confess his sin, usually on his knees, before the community, when the Abbot would prescribe either absolution or that he was to be disciplined, which, if it was a severe penalty, might involve exile. Dr W. Reeves in the preface to his biography of Adomnan, published in 1874, emphasised that 'All the members of the community, as well as the affiliated monasteries, were, by their monastic vow, bound to yield prompt and implicit obedience to the Abbot of the Mother Church, who was termed holy father and holy senior.'

The daily round of prescribed duty was for the benefit and spiritual well-being of the community. It was a hard life, particularly for the Working Brothers, who would also have had to contend with the variable climate. However, it must have given them endless opportunities to observe nature even when occupied with monastic duties, and it is not difficult to imagine that in time, given this close relationship between nature and themselves, they might have identified Iona as the real monastery surrounded by the *vallum* of the sea with the sky as their spiritual mantle. The love of nature is a distinctive feature of Celtic Christianity and it is echoed in the religious artefacts of the period, its form deriving from the art of the La Tène culture,

9 Cocks and hens, interlinear ornament, Book of Kells, *folio 67r*

which, although it declined under Roman domination in Britain and the Continent of Europe, continued in Ireland during the early centuries of the first millennium.

It is now generally accepted that a part if not the whole of the *Book of Kells* was created on Iona, possibly to celebrate the bicentenary of the death of St Columba, but inevitably taking far longer to complete than was anticipated. (It is now in Trinity College Library, Dublin.) One of the artists of the *Book of Kells* provides delightful grace-notes to the manuscript pages with his illustrations of mice, cocks, cats, a goat and guinea-fowl that range through the intertwining foliage of the illuminated text. There is a sense of the small incidents of nature continuing without the interruption of worldly events, echoing the daily life of the monastery surrounded by the earth, sea and sky. This was the Celtic Church's inspiration and their domain.

St Oran's Chapel

There is, for me, an element of sanctity in the oldest surviving building on Iona, St Oran's Chapel, which stands within the burial-ground of St Oran's Churchyard. The chapel was dedicated to Oran, a cousin of St Columba, and is thought to have been built as a mortuary chapel by either Somerled, Lord of the Isles, or by his son Reginald in the twelfth century. The style of the chapel resembles Irish stone buildings of that period, based in plan form upon that of the early Celtic churches or oratories, which were originally constructed of timber with roofs of rushes or shingles. These buildings were described in the old Irish Behon Laws, a commentary written after 1010, and their dimensions are referred to as being on average 15 ft × 10 ft or in a proportion of 1.5 : 1. It is tempting to speculate on the possibility that St Oran's Chapel was built on the original site of St Columba's Oratory, since the proportions are similar. Magnus Barelegs, King of Norway, in an expedition to the Western Isles in 1098, visited 'the small church of Columcille' on Iona, which suggests that there was still a monastic community on the island in the eleventh century. It has been argued that he was referring to St Columba's Shrine which forms part òf the Abbey. But it would have been too small to have served as an oratory, and it is of the wrong proportion, being almost square in plan. St Oran's Chapel has been restored by the Iona Community, work being completed in 1957.

The Benedictine Abbey

The original Benedictine Abbey, of which the present structure is the completed reconstruction of a later fifteenth-century building, was founded in 1200 by Reginald, son of Somerled. Although the reasons for its foundation are unknown, its establishment was presumably approved by the Somerled family since the endowment included not only Iona but also land on the islands of Mull, Colonsay, Canna and Islay as well as part of Lorn on the mainland. However, clearly one intention in locating the Abbey on Iona was the hope that the Benedictine order might inherit the reputation that had been gained by successive Christian churches on the site of the first Columban monastery. This continuity of location was also maintained in the name of the Abbey, which, although it had been dedicated to the Virgin Mary, was known universally as the monastery of St Columba. There is also a certain significance in the precise location of the building which appears to have been constructed on the foundations of earlier structures and adjacent to the existing St Columba's Shrine. The secular part of the Abbey, the claustral buildings, are on the north side of the church and not on the south, which is the more usual arrangement. This was governed by the need of running water for sanitation but the Abbey could equally as well have been sited to the north of the stream, which would have enabled a traditional plan to have been followed.

The prosperity of the Abbey throughout the thirteenth century is reflected in the extended programme of building work which was disrupted for almost a century as a result of internal dissension and external interference in governance of the Abbey by the MacKinnon family. However, from 1450 reconstruction and new work got under way and was to continue until the end of the fifteenth century. The fall of the Lords of the Isles and the arrival of the Reformation in Scotland altered the status of the Abbey but it continued to maintain its spiritual leadership in the Western Isles. A change of policy occurred, however, in 1499, when, after petitioning by the Campbell Duke of Argyll, the Pope granted the abbacy of Iona to the Bishop of the Isles, without the appointed Bishop having to take the Benedictine habit.

Charles I's Act of Revocation in 1625 attempted to restore to the church the pre-Reformation ownership of its land and titles. This resulted in the Macleans of Duart being ordered by the King in 1635 to return ownership of Iona to the Bishop and contribute towards the restoration of the Abbey. When the Scottish Covenanters in 1638 called for the excommunication and deposing of all bishops, the Prayer Book to be abolished, and a Committee to be created to investigate abuses, in direct opposition to the King's wishes, this provided the Macleans with an opportunity to depose the Bishop of Iona, Neil Campbell, and take hereditary control of the island. Thus, in 1638, ended 1075 years of a continuing line of what each appointed Abbot had claimed to be 'a successor of Columba'.

After this the Abbey gradually fell into ruin. The ownership of the island passed from the Macleans of Duart to that of the Dukes of Argyll after the Jacobite Rising of 1689. They retained possession of it until it was bought by the Sir Hugh Fraser Foundation in 1979 for the National Trust for Scotland. However, the eighth Duke of Argyll, having instigated a policy of restoration referred to earlier, made a gift of the Abbey and nunnery to the Church of Scotland. In accord with the Duke's wishes the re-building of the Abbey Church continued and was completed in 1910. As the Duke had excluded the local parish minister from involvement in the trusteeship and as the local community had their own parish church it was not possible for many years to reach agreement as to what purpose the Abbey could serve.

The Iona Community

In 1938, a scheme was proposed which led to the formation of the Iona Community. George MacLeod – who, in the First World War, had served as a Captain in the Argyll & Sutherland Highlanders and been decorated with the Military Cross and the Croix de Guerre – resigned as minister of Govan Old Parish Church on Clydeside in that year to create the Community at

10 Restored tower, choir and south aisle, 1904–8

the age of thirty-three. He left Govan with twelve craftsmen and young ministers to settle on the island with the intention of re-building the secular part of the Abbey which had not been restored by the Church of Scotland. It was not a propitious time to undertake such work. Unemployment, the lack of funds for reconstruction and the onset of the Second World War inevitably delayed progress. The work of restoration continued throughout the war to such effect that in 1956 – a full century after the visit of Prince Albert – Queen Elizabeth, The Duke of Edinburgh, Princess Margaret and others attended service in the Abbey at which George MacLeod preached; it was the first visit on the island by a sovereign since the reign in the eleventh century of Malcolm Canmore. Restoration continued during the 1950s and 1960s to be finally completed in 1967 when George MacLeod retired as leader of the Community at the age of seventy-two – but now as the Very Reverend Lord MacLeod of Fuinary.

The principles of the Iona Community were explained by MacLeod in his book *We Shall Rebuild* (1944; revised 1962). The intention of the Community was not only to rebuild the Abbey buildings as a symbol of faith in the unity of worship and work, a conjunction of the spiritual and material, but also to create on Iona a base from which to take the ideas which they had formulated to the outside world. Ministers were sent to housing estates and factories to experiment with new ways of promoting Christianity. Young people became interested in this approach and visited Iona, resulting in youth camps being created on the island which have subsequently become an important part of the work of the Community. Membership has grown over the years and there is now an interdenominational fraternity of 3800 friends and associates working in many parts of the world. The intention of its members is not to create a new monastic order but to work together in normal daily life, committing themselves to the work of the community and maintaining 'a common discipline of life'. To this end they follow a five-part Rule which has evolved since the inception of the Community. This Rule includes time spent each day in prayer and study; donating a small percentage of their income towards the Community, charitable organisations and their local church; accounting for their use of time in recreation and family ties; regular meetings with other members including involvement in the administration of the Community; and perhaps most importantly, pledging to work towards peace and justice at both national and international levels. This Rule thus provides a means of binding the Community together in common purpose, enabling them individually and collectively to bridge the void between Christian belief and the material world in which we and they live. It was the original intention of George MacLeod that only by discovering alternative ways of living and working together could the Church make Christianity relevant to people in an industrial age. It still remains the vision which directs the work of the Community from one generation to the next.

MacLeod Centre

A visible sign of this can be seen on the site of the original residential buildings which have now been demolished to be replaced by the new MacLeod Centre, which will provide accommodation for young people, families and for those who are disabled. Many people over the years have made a pilgrimage to Iona to share the life of the Community at the Abbey and as the site formerly housed only the Residential Youth Centre it was considered important to extend the offer of the facilities which a new building could provide to all age groups. Entries were invited for an international architectural competition to discover the most suitable design for the site, and an English firm's design, that of Seilden & Clegg Design from Bath, was considered the most appropriate, and currently (1986) the Iona Community are raising funds to implement the project. The location of the new building is to the west of the Abbey on the far side of *Cnoc nan Carnan*, Hill of the Rocks, and is on a central axis between the two crosses which stand at the entrance to the Abbey, dedicated to St John and St Martin. The former is undergoing repair and a replica stands on the original base, while the latter is original. They both date from the eighth century while a third cross between the two, of which only the remnants of the shaft remain, is St Matthew's Cross and is of ninth- or tenth-century origin. St Martin's Cross is of particular interest because there is a representation of the Virgin and Child surrounded by angels that closely resembles a similar image in the *Book of Kells*, which suggests that at least one of the artists of the *Book of Kells* was aware of the details of the cross on Iona in the eighth century.

11 The Virgin and Child with Angels, Book of Kells, *folio 7v*

27

The Spirit of Columba's Isle

If you now continue your walk from the Abbey, past *Torr Abb*, across the road and then over the earthworks of the remaining fragment of the *vallum* towards the west along the ancient causeway which was formerly the southern bank of what was once Lochan Mor, then you will again be free of the constraints of history, of places, and even of people. If you are fortunate it will be one of those summer days on the island which are both idyllic and memorable: idyllic because Iona will come close to the Celtic description of heaven, as portrayed in the anonymously written *The Islands of Earthly Paradise*: 'There is an island far away, around which the sea-horses glisten, flowing on their white course against its shining shape; four pillows support it.'

Memorable because you will become aware in the still air of the scents of flowers in season: of wild thyme, milkwort, stork's-bill, rose-root, lovage and thrift, all of which may be found on the island. As the forgiving turf consents to your every step you will also become conscious of the sensuous quality that Iona possesses which intertwines nature with human existence, and which is so often referred to in Celtic poetry, with its underlying belief in the earth goddess of pre-Christian religions. To the west you will glimpse the Atlantic and as you move towards the western shore of the island you will find a circle of stones midway on your journey which are the only remains of a hermit's cell and where there is a stillness, if you are fortunate to be alone, which is for me unlike any other part of the island. When you finally leave you will find that your natural inclination will lead you towards the ocean, which, as you approach, will gradually intrude upon the silence, as the waves, in perpetual collision with the rock-laden shore resound like organ music on the dark side of the sun.

The rocks of Iona are little older than the ocean from which they rise. The Reverend Edward Craig Trenholme in *The Story of Iona* (1909) has written: 'When our planet, from a glowing mass of combustion like the sun, shrivelled into a globe with a solid crust and the first oceans condensed in the hollows of its hot surface – then it was that the Archaean rocks, of which Iona and the Outer Hebrides consist, were formed on the sea bottom. They contain no fossils, for, as far as is known, no living creatures as yet existed in the desolate waste of waters or on the primeval land. They are hard, rugged and twisted, and in Iona as elsewhere marble had been developed by the vast heat and pressure they have undergone.'

On Iona the rocks are always with you for they are only partly hidden by a thin veneer of turf and heather and you can sense their antiquity when your path is impeded by the presence of their implacable solidity. To fully appreciate the age of this part of the earth's surface you must climb to the summit of Dun I and survey the surrounding terrain. That early settlers were prepared to live in this remote and primeval part of the world appears perverse but there is some evidence that ancient rocks possessed magical qualities for the old religions; and Iona, for this reason, may have been chosen as a centre by the Druids for their rituals. It is thought that Dun I may possibly have been used for their primitive rites and it is not difficult to imagine, when standing on such a commanding site, that it would have appeared to them to have been the centre of the world.

The White Sands of Iona

The early Celtic Church, particularly in Ireland, adopted many elements of the pagan traditions of pre-Christian worship and subsumed its mythology with the new faith; not least of which was a love of nature that found expression in poetry that is laden with images of the natural world. Many of the poems attributed to Columba describe nature in striking detail. On many occasions throughout his life on Iona he must have climbed Dun I to contemplate the world about him. In old age when this was no longer possible, Columba became a frequent visitor to the north headland of the island; he would climb *Cnoc an Suidhe*, Hill of the Seat, and gaze out to sea beyond the white sands that form beaches around the shores of this part of Iona. These dazzling white sands and the quality of the light have appealed to painters, such as the Scottish Colourists S. J. Peploe (1871–1935) and F. C. B. Cadell (1883–1937).

That simple faith in the unity of all forms of life with Mother Earth would appear one and a half thousand years later to have a scientific basis, which our sceptical age may just possibly be prepared to accept. Dr James Lovelock, a British scientist formerly working for the American space agency NASA, has proposed a theory known as the Gaia Hypothesis, which suggests 'that the physical and chemical condition of the surface of the Earth, of the atmosphere and of the oceans has been and is actually made fit and comfortable by the presence of life itself'.

One small but significant particle of evidence, among all the other facts which support this theory, is to be found in the sand which forms the north headland of Iona. The white sand consists of coccolithopore shells of calcium carbonate that each winter are blown across the island and deposited on the fields, thus enriching the soil in the process. The coccolithopores are single-celled protista some $1/200$ mm in diameter that live in the sunlit upper layers of the ocean. Contained within their shells is a drop of oil which acts both as a food store and to maintain equilibrium in the sea. When they die they sink to the seabed forming a burial-ground of carbon dioxide. To provide tolerable temperatures on earth the carbon dioxide layer in the atmosphere must be maintained at an optimum density, otherwise a 'greenhouse' effect would result with the sun's rays entering through the layer but being unable to escape. A process that begins with all living plants drawing down carbon dioxide from the atmosphere and, through their decay, forming an acid in the moist earth transforms the silicate particles in the soil to bicarbonate. This is transported by rainwater through streams which eventually flow into the sea and is then finally used by the coccolithopores to form their shells.

The movement of vast shoals of coccolithopores was first confirmed in 1980 from a satellite in space when, on a modified wavelength, they were revealed as a large white shape north-west of Stornoway on Lewis. Subsequent sightings have been made establishing this collective movement in the sea, with the evidence of their existence revealed on the white sands of beaches such as those on Iona where the sea has deposited the shells that have not settled in a sedimentary layer on the seabed.

When the earth is compared with other planets in the solar system it becomes apparent that we are unique. What is notable is that we have a stable atmosphere which provides a life-support system that contradicts the known evidence of planetary processes, suggesting that there is a regulatory system to maintain equilibrium.

As Dr Lovelock has expressed it: 'The concept of Mother Earth or, as the Greeks called her long ago, Gaia, has been widely held throughout history and has been the basis of a belief which still coexists with the great religions. As a result of the accumulation of evidence about the natural environment and the growth of the science of ecology, there have recently been speculations that the biosphere may be more than just the complete range of all living things within their natural habitat of soil, sea, and air. Ancient belief and modern knowledge have fused emotionally in the awe with which astronauts with their own eyes and we by indirect vision have seen the Earth revealed in all its shining beauty against the deep darkness of space.'

As a coda to this modern interpretation of the earth goddess there is a traditional folk charm in the *Carmina Gadelica* of which Columba would surely have approved: 'May I be an island in the sun, may I be a hill on the land, may I be a star when the moon wanes, may I be a staff to the weak one...'

Further Reading

Anderson, A. O. and M. O. (ed.), *Life of St Columba* (Adomnan), London, 1961.

Argyll, 8th Duke of, *Iona*, London, 1871.

Boswell, James, *Journal of a Tour to the Hebrides with Samuel Johnson, LL D*, London, 1773.

Carmichael, Dr Alexander (ed. & tr.), *Carmina Gadelica*, 4 vols, Edinburgh, 1928. Hymns and incantations; illustrative notes on words, rites and customs, dying and obsolete, orally collected in the Highlands and Islands of Scotland.

Chadwick, Nora, *The Celts*, Harmondsworth, 1970.

Craig, Maurice, *The Architecture of Ireland*, London, 1982.

Dunbar, John G., and Fisher, Ian, *Iona*, Edinburgh, 1983.

Finlay, Ian, *Columba*, London, 1979.

Henry, Françoise (ed.), *The Book of Kells*, London, 1974.

Huyshe, Wentworth (ed.), *Life of St Columba* (Adomnan), London, 1905.

Jackson, Kenneth, *A Celtic Miscellany*, Harmondsworth, 1951.

Lovelock, J. E., *Gaia: A New Look at Life on Earth*, Oxford, 1979; rev. edn., 1982.

Maclean, Lachlan, *A Historical Account of Iona*, Edinburgh, 1833.

MacLeod, George, *We Shall Rebuild*, Iona Community, Glasgow, 1944; rev. edn., 1962.

McNeill, F. Marian (ed.), *An Iona Anthology*, Edinburgh, 1947.

Macphail, J. R. W. (ed.), *Highland Papers of Donald Gregory* (1674), 5 vols, Scottish History Society, Glasgow, 1914.

Macquarrie, Alan, *Iona through the Ages*, Isle of Coll, Argyll, 1983.

Murray, Sarah, *The Beauties of Scotland*, London, 1799.

Pennant, Thomas, *A Tour in Scotland and Voyage to the Hebrides*, London, 1772.

Reeves, W. (ed.), *Life of St Columba* (Adomnan), Edinburgh, 1874.

Skene, W. F., *Celtic Scotland*, 3 vols, Edinburgh, 1886.

Smyth, Alfred, *Warlords and Holy Men*, London, 1984.

Trenholme, Rev. Edward Craig, *The Story of Iona*, Edinburgh, 1909.

IONa

We were now treading that illustrious Island, which was once the luminary of the Caledonian regions, whence savage clans and roving barbarians derived the benefits of knowledge, and the blessings of religion. To abstract the mind from all local emotion would be impossible, if it were endeavoured, and would be foolish if it were possible. Whatever withdraws us from the power of our senses, whatever makes the past, the distant, or the future, predominate over the present, advances us in the dignity of thinking beings. Far from me, and from my friends, be such frigid philosophy as may conduct us indifferent and unmoved over any ground which has been dignified by wisdom, bravery or virtue. That man is little to be envied, whose patriotism would not gain force upon the plain of *Marathon*, or whose piety would not grow warmer among the ruins of *Iona*.

Dr Samuel Johnson
19 October 1773

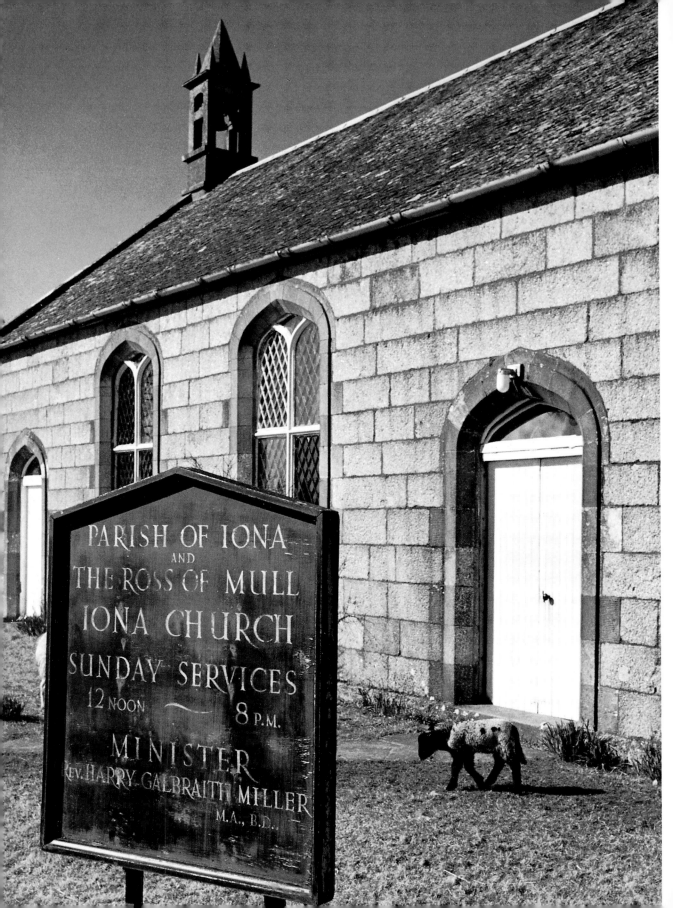

Photographs